Selfishly Unselfish

You Matter

K.R. Sharp

Copyright © 2023 by K.R. Sharp

Dedication

My family, whom I always miss. My kids, who never cease to amaze me, I am blessed to have you with me after long years of separation.

In memory of
My beloved parents

To you who read my book. Your interest in my work profoundly humbles me, and I want to thank you for your dedication to the story. Your support has been invaluable, and I cannot thank you enough for your enthusiasm and encouragement.

Connect with the author through
email: krsreads@gmail.com or Instagram
@krsreads

Book Description

What if we could reclaim our peace, joy, and happiness? What if we could break free from the chains that bind us and live on our terms?

Amidst the chaos and the strife, we often lose sight of what makes us come alive. We forget who we are and let life's trials and tribulations define us. But what if we could take back our power?

Prepare to be inspired, uplifted, and encouraged by the pages of this book. Selfishly unselfish is different from your average read. Its words are not just ink on paper but a call to action to chase your dreams, push beyond your limits, and take advantage of this opportunity to transform your life and unleash your full potential—a roadmap to personal growth and self-discovery. With every turn of the page, you'll feel a surge of motivation, a burst of encouragement, and a renewed sense of empowerment.

Indulge yourself in a delightful collection of poems that will captivate your heart and inspire you. This book is a treasure trove of emotions you will easily relate to. You'll find yourself transported to a world of relatable feelings and experiences that will deeply resonate with you whether you're looking for a moment of solace or want to dive into the beauty of language. Each page contains verses that will leave a lasting impression on your heart and soul. So, get ready to embark on a journey of self-discovery as you explore the depths of your emotions through the art of poetry.

Contents

Introduction

Are you tired of living a life that doesn't align with your dreams and aspirations? Do you feel stuck in a rut and don't know how to move forward? Empowerment for life is the key to unlocking your potential and taking control of your future. It's about recognizing your strengths and abilities, setting goals, taking risks, and making changes. Empowerment for life is not just a concept, it's a mindset that can lead to a more fulfilling and successful life. So, are you ready to take the challenge and create a meaningful and satisfying life?

Imagine waking up every day with a sense of purpose and direction, knowing exactly what you want to achieve and having the motivation to make it happen. That's the power of motivation. The spark ignites the fire of success and drives us toward our goals. But motivation alone is not enough. We also need empowerment - the fuel that keeps our fire burning. Empowerment gives people the power and resources to take control of their lives and make their own decisions. Motivation and empowerment form a powerful combination that can help us achieve anything we set our minds to.

Life is a beautiful journey, but it's also filled with obstacles that make us feel stuck. However, it's time to take control and pave our paths toward the life we have always envisioned. With determination, resilience, and compassion, we can conquer any setback and triumph over any challenge that comes our way. It's time to break free from the shackles of monotony and take control of our lives. With determination, resilience, and compassion, we can conquer any challenge that crosses our path. It's time to embark on a journey of self-discovery, where we break down barriers and start living the life we have always imagined. Let's make the most of every moment and create a future we can be proud of.

One

It's okay to take it slow, at your own pace.

Picture

When you think of love, a picture that comes into your mind is wonderful and pleasant. Yes, love is a beautiful feeling you're expecting at some point in your life. Few came and gave a little glow and joy; some passed by to teach lessons. However, we agree that it needs work on both sides. Merely love is the risk of disappointment and frustration that would be about to happen at the drop of a hat. It's a continuous pour of energy which is great though it can sometimes be exhausting. On a positive note, giving is more fulfilling, though don't forget to care for yourself first. Remember that you can only give what you have to others. So, love yourself first and others without expectations.

When thoughts of love come drifting by,
A picture forms in heart and eye,

Of tenderness, of joy and peace,
A feeling that will never cease.

For love is a wondrous, pleasant thing,
The beauty of which we all do sing,
It's something we all hope to find,
A treasure of the heart and mind.

Yet love is not a simple game,
It needs effort, work, and mutual aim,
For though it brings us great delight,
It also holds the risk of fright.

Disappointment and frustration too,
Can come at any moment, it's true,
But love demands a constant pour,
Of energy that we must explore.
It's a tiring journey, we must admit,
But giving love is what makes us fit,
For through it all, we learn to thrive,
And keep the flame of love alive.

Still, in giving love, we must be wise,
And care for ourselves, lest our feelings die,
For what we give to others we must first possess,
Lest our love be empty, without finesse.

So, love yourself first, do not forget,
And then to others, your love beget,
For in loving, we find the key,
To unlock the heart and set it free.

Choices

Hold on, don't sell yourself short just because you don't have your other half at the moment. This is the time when you can have as many choices as you want without being guilty of anyone's approval. Immerse yourself instead of the moments you can do without anyone interrupting your silence. It can open up the inner wonders you have wished for. Explore the depths of your soul and quench your thirst for independence and liberation. It strengthens your will to pursue things you've wanted to accomplish. You start to plan about the desires you want in your life—this time with focus and direction. So, keep still.

In the stillness of solitude,
There is wonder to behold,
A chance to immerse oneself,
In stories yet untold.

For though the heart may yearn,
For a love to call its own,
There is freedom in the waiting,
A chance to be alone.

To explore the depths within,
And quench a thirst for truth,
To strengthen will and purpose,
And plan for future's youth.

So hold on, dear one, hold tight,
And don't sell yourself short,
For in this time of solitude,
There is beauty to exhort.

Embrace the choices you can make,
Without guilt or approval's sway,
And in the silence of your heart,
You'll find the words to say.

Words of hope and courage,
Of independence and liberation,
A roadmap for the future,
With focus and direction.

So keep still, dear one, keep still,
And let your heart take flight,
For in the stillness of your soul,
There is a world of light.

Watch Yourself

Here you are, wondering the what ifs or if only. Nevertheless, watch yourself every day. You're doing perfectly okay and even more confident in yourself. It seems like yesterday you were dreading being where you are now. It's like a dream come true. You have all the control over the life you've always wanted. You are gradually pushing the wishes to come true and navigate the greatest love towards yourself. You're utterly beyond being fine.

Oh, wandering mind, so full of doubt
Your thoughts run rampant, always about
What could have been, or what may be
But here and now is all you need to see

Watch yourself each and every day
You're doing fine, in every way
Confidence radiates from within
A newfound strength, where to begin?

It feels like just yesterday
You were lost, unsure of the way
But now, it's like a dream come true
All your hard work, paying dues

You have the power, the control
To shape your life, reach your goal

Pushing wishes, making them real
Guiding yourself, with hands on the wheel

The love you give, the greatest of all
Towards yourself, you stand tall
Becoming more, with each passing day
A force to be reckoned with, in every way

So here you are, in this moment in time
A masterpiece, a work so divine
Beyond being fine, you shine so bright
May your light guide you, through every night.

Right Track

Days pass quickly, and you don't notice the bad memories fade away slowly. The pain in your chest doesn't hurt that much anymore. You're on the right track to healing. The times you're holding in your mind disappear into fragments of thoughts. Here's a new time to add value to your existence, never take yourself for granted. Pick a new hobby or learn something that interests you and moves your soul. If you're tired, take a rest and listen to your body. It is always good to start now rather than look back with guilt and ask yourself why you haven't started then. It's time to turn the page and start a new chapter. It is never too late.

Days pass by quickly, as if on wings they fly
And soon enough, the bad memories die T
he pain in your chest that once brought you to your knees
Slowly fades and loses its ability to squeeze

You're on the right track of healing, moving ahead
The times that once pained you, now just fragments in your head
A new day has dawned, a time to add value to your existence
Never take yourself for granted, embrace your persistence

Pick a new hobby or learn something that moves your soul
Open new doors and reach for new goals
When you're tired, take a break and rest
Listen to your body, it knows best

It's always good to start now, and not wait until then
So you won't look back with guilt and ask why you didn't begin
It's time to turn the page and start a new chapter
It's never too late, don't let time be a captor

Embrace each day, and all that it brings
The highs and lows, the joys and stings
Find your purpose, your passion, your drive
Live your life fully, and come alive.

Neglect Arises

Happiness comes from within. Yes, it feels good if you have someone to share with. Nonetheless, seeking it from others could become frustrating if neglect arises. Than becoming attached to anything or anyone, it is best to create a deeper connection within and treat yourself with the most respect and love you can possibly give. Indeed, you can't give what you don't have. So, start with yourself.

Happiness Comes From Within

A notion oft repeated,
Happiness comes from within,
A truth that bears repeating,
In a world that thrives on sin.

Yes, it feels good to share,
Joy with those we love,
But seeking it from others,
Can lead to frustration and mistrust.

Neglect can arise,
When we rely on external sources,
But seeking happiness within,
Can lead to deeper, stronger forces.

Attachments can be fleeting,
And can cause pain and strife,
But treating ourselves with love and respect,
Can result in a fulfilling life.

Indeed, we can't give,
What we don't have to start,
So, we must begin with ourselves,
And nurture our own heart.

Create a deeper connection,
Within your very core,
And let it radiate outwards,
Into a world that craves more.

Happiness comes from within,
And that's where it should begin,
So, love yourself and treat yourself well,
And let your happiness never dim.

Desire is Powerful

To seek what you desire is powerful. Everything around you would shift to different avenues of opportunity. However, be careful to only jump into such with a thorough assessment. For the heart can blind the mind, and the flowery words can blur out logical reasoning. You are wiser now, gullible looking, but strength is within you. Previous experiences taught you higher levels of wisdom.

To seek what you desire is a power to behold,
A force that can shift every path you unfold,
Opportunities abound, all around you they lie,
But be careful to assess before you jump and try.

For the heart, oh the heart, can be a blinding sight,
And it can easily obscure the mind's logical might,
Those flowery words can wrap you in their sweet embrace,
And you can end up lost in a confusing maze.

But fear not, dear seeker, for you are wiser now,
And your strength is within, you just have to avow,
Previous experiences have taught you much wisdom,
And that knowledge is your guide to a better kingdom.

So go forth, and seek what your heart truly desires,
But remember to assess, to avoid any burning fires,

You are gullible-looking, a trait that's often misunderstood,
But with your new-found wisdom, you're stronger than you
ever thought you could.

Real Meaning

The fast dynamics of friendship and relationships can overtake the real meaning of it. Shallow connections and phony attachments are not real. They are there to add small joys and fun, although you only have yourself in the long term. Don't wait for others to appreciate you; thus, be grateful for the things you have gone through. You have yourself to thank for.

The fast dynamics of friendship and love,
Can overwhelm and leave us in a shove,
The meaning of it all can become obscured,
Hidden by the excitement that has occurred.

Shallow connections and phony attachments,
Can lead us down a path of false fulfillment,
We chase after small joys and cheap thrills,
Only to find that it was not the real deal.

In the long term, it is ourselves we have,
To rely on, to trust, to find a path,
Don't wait for others to appreciate,
The journey you've taken, the choices you've made.

Be grateful for the things you've gone through,
For they have shaped and molded you,
You have yourself to thank for the growth,
That has come from overcoming both highs and lows.

So cherish those connections, both deep and true,
For they can bring joy and meaning, yes it's true,
But don't forget the importance of self-love,
For it's the foundation that all else is built above.

It was You

Underrated recognition of what you have endured is betrayal towards oneself. Remember, it was you who sat in pain, cried the tears, gathered the broken pieces, and pushed yourself to become stronger than before. You owe everything to yourself. That was how it molded you into the unique person you are now. Unapologetically you.

Underrated recognition of what you have endured
Is betrayal towards oneself, so stay assured
That you, my dear, are the one who sat in pain
And cried the tears that fell like heavy rain

You gathered the broken pieces, one by one
And pushed yourself to become stronger than before, well done
It was your strength that carried you through the storm
And it's your resilience that kept you warm

You owe everything to yourself, don't forget
The hard work that you put in, and the tears you've wept
It's how you've become the unique person you are now
So be unapologetically you, and take a bow

For you are the one who has overcome
*And shown the world what you're made of, what you've
become*

So don't let anyone else take credit for your hard work
For you're the one who's faced the challenges, and didn't shirk

Underrated recognition of your journey is a shame
*For you've faced the struggles, and come out stronger, that's
your claim to fame*
So always remember, you are the one who's endured
And you owe everything to yourself, that's for sure.

Strange

Risk is not new to you. You have tried them all, yet even the fear did not stop you from wanting the change you eagerly hoped for. Strange that you were able to get through. Nevertheless, you did, which makes you extraordinary. You don't need anyone to validate you because you know your worth deep down.

Risk is not new to you,
You've been there before,
Tried them all with bravery,
And never once did you ignore.

The fear may have lingered,
But it didn't stop your drive,
For change was what you sought,
And with passion, you did strive.

It's strange how you made it through,
But you did it all the same,
And that's what makes you unique,
A person of extraordinary aim.

You don't need validation,
For you know your worth inside,
And with every step you take,
Your self-confidence does abide.

So hold your head up high,
And face the risks that come your way,

For you've proven time and time again,
That nothing can stand in your way.

Keep pushing forward with courage,
And let your spirit soar,
For you are a force to be reckoned with,
And your potential is endless galore.

Crumble

You cared too much. The concern, tears, and words were overflowing. However, did you get back what you deserved? The world has a funny way of teaching lessons. You've learned to drop it, let go, and move on. You thought it would crumble your world.

You cared so much, your heart overflowed
With concern, tears, and words untold
Yet did you get back what you deserved?
The world's lessons can be quite absurd

It's funny how life can teach and mold
The things we thought we knew so well, they unfold
The pain that comes with caring too much
Leaves scars on the heart that stay as such

You've learned to drop it, let it go
And move on from what you thought you'd know
For the weight of the world can be so heavy
It can crumble your world, make it unsteady

But you are strong, you push through
You take the lessons and make them anew
For in the end, it's not the caring that was wrong
But the expectations that we hold on for too long

So drop it, let go, and move on
The world will keep spinning long after you're gone
And in the end, the only thing that will remain
Are the memories of love and the lessons from pain.

Stopped Counting

Some things are better left unsaid, for you've resented and made yourself heard once, twice, thrice, and stopped counting—no chance of you being listened to, which is one of the deepest pains to deal with. The happiness you thought someone could give you was just a joke, after all, when the day you woke up and just decided to make yourself your person. It brought back all the control in your life.

Some things are better left unsaid,
For words can fall upon deaf ears;
Resentment festers and fills your head,
And all you feel is pain and tears.

You've spoken out, once and twice,
Thrice and more, but still no heed;
Your heart is filled with pain and strife,
And all you want is to be freed.

The happiness you thought you'd find,
In someone else, was just a dream;
You woke up one day with a new mind,
And felt the power of self-esteem.

You took control and found your voice,
You made yourself your own best friend;
You learned to live without the noise,
And your life found a peaceful end.

So sometimes it's best to keep quiet,
To let the silence speak for you;
To find the strength deep inside it,
And be the person you always knew.

Complacent

It feels good to hold on to something you thought was good for you. However, it turned sour and complacent. The load on you is getting heavier each time, ignored and uncomplimented. How rude; you've learned your lesson the bitter way. And it is your promise to yourself that you would only give your energy to whom it is worth it. Nevertheless, value you as a person, for you are lovable and deserve the love you give in return.

In the beginning, it felt so right
To hold on to what was in sight
A sweet promise, a shining light
It seemed like an endless delight

But as time passed, it turned so sour
The weight grew heavy by the hour
It became a burden too much to bear
A load that no one else would share

Yet still, you tried to hold on tight
Ignoring the pain with all your might
Hoping that it would all turn out right
But it never did, despite your fight

How rude it was to treat you so
To leave you stranded and alone to go
You learned your lesson in the bitterest way
That some things aren't meant to stay

But you made a promise to yourself
That you would only give your energy to those who help
Who value you and cherish your worth
Who see the beauty in you since your birth

It's time to stop holding onto what's wrong
And start valuing yourself all along
You are lovable and deserve the love you give
And this is the life you deserve to live

Home

You are trying hard to build connections with others because the purpose of life is to care. However, don't forget to protect your heart. Some people might not be ready to accept what you offer, and it's not your responsibility to change them. Be yourself, for home is not the place or another person. It is you; you can feel it in your heart.

In life's intricate weave of threads,
We strive to connect with those ahead,
To care for others, our purpose clear,
And spread love, far and near.

But in our quest to forge those ties,
We must not forget to be wise,
And guard our hearts, lest they break,
From those who cannot reciprocate.

For some may not be ready or willing,
To accept the love we are giving,
It's not our job to change their ways,
But to be true to ourselves, always.

Home is not a place or person,
It's a feeling that we can summon,
From within our hearts, so pure and strong,
A sense of belonging that keeps us on.

So, as we navigate this world of ours,
Let's build connections, spread love like flowers,
But never forget to protect our heart,
For it's the essence of who we are, part by part.

Comparison

Realize that comparing yourself to everyone can leave you vain or bitter. There's no comparison between the sun and the moon. They shine when it's their time. Everyone has something good to bring to the table. Focusing on learning, growing, and building a contented life are the critical key to happiness. Know that you're unique in your way. It's all about believing in yourself. Appreciate who you are. You are enough.

In life, we often find ourselves,
Comparing to those around, T
he endless game of competition,
One that can leave us quite unbound.

For when we measure ourselves,
Against others, far and near,
We may find ourselves quite vain,
Or bitter, filled with fear.

It's important to remember,
That we are all unique and bright,
Like the sun and moon up high,
We each shine in our own right.

No need to compare, my friends,
For we each have our own place,
We all bring something to the table,
A gift that can't be replaced.

So focus on your own journey,
On learning, growing, and building,
For a contented life is found,
When your own path you're fulfilling.

Believe in yourself, dear one,
For you are enough, and more,
Appreciate who you are,
And your own unique gifts adore.

No need to compare or compete,
For you are one of a kind,
Embrace your individuality,
And true happiness you'll find.

Privileged

Breathe; you have to feel it before it heals. Trust that it will soon be over, and you'll have the inner peace you have wanted for so long. You're privileged to reach where you are, which someone else is praying for. You're much better than you were years ago. Continue with your progress; you never know whom you're inspiring.

Breathe deep, my dear, and feel the air
That flows into your lungs with care I
t's a reminder that you're alive
And the world around you will survive

You've been through trials and pain
But you're still standing, don't refrain
From trusting that it will soon be over
And you'll have the inner peace you've sought after

The road has not been easy, it's true
But you've made progress, and that's a breakthrough
You're in a place that others pray to be
And you should be proud of what you've achieved

Keep moving forward, step by step
And know that you're an inspiration, don't forget

Your journey has been long and hard
But you're stronger now than you were at the start

And as you breathe, you heal and grow
The pain will lessen, and the light will show
So trust in yourself and in the road ahead
For you're capable of amazing things, it's said

Breathe deep, my dear, and let it all out
The doubts, the fears, the pain, the clout
You're on your way to inner peace
And with each breath, your progress will increase.

New Chapter

There comes a day when you realize that moving where you are stuck would be the best relief you could ever do. Deep down, you know that it is not working and that you need a change in your life to be of purpose and follow what your heart desires. You know there's so much more to your book of life than the page you are stuck on. It's the start of a new chapter, write it well.

In the depths of your soul lies a truth,
A realization that's been brewing since youth,
That where you are now is a place of stuck,
And the relief you need is to move, oh what luck!

For as you look around and take stock,
You see that what you have is not what you'd choose to rock,
And though it's tough to leave the familiar behind,
Your heart whispers to you, it's time to unwind.

With this knowledge, a new energy springs forth,
A hope that was hidden, now revealed in full force,
The understanding that to be of purpose,
You must leave behind what's not working, no need to fuss.

For there's a world of possibilities out there,
A vast horizon begging for you to dare,

To follow your heart, to chase your dreams,
And create a life that beams.

And though it may be scary, this new start,
Remember that you hold the pen to your life's chart,
It's a fresh page, a new chapter to write,
So go ahead and let your spirit ignite.

For you are the author of your book of life,
The protagonist in this tale, with all its strife,
So take that first step with courage and grace,
And write a story that leaves a lasting trace.

Hell and Back

Since everything is temporary and uncertain, be prepared for countless heartaches. There are lots of things you cannot control. Have a humble heart and accept it. It would make everything so much easier. Trust that you can handle what life throws at you because you have already gone through hell and back. And yes, you survived. You are still standing and ever strong.

In life, we journey through a path unknown
And face countless heartaches, all on our own
For everything's temporary and uncertain
We must accept and be ready, no need to burden

There's much that we cannot control
But we can shape our heart and soul
To be humble, to be strong
And to hold on, when everything goes wrong

We must trust in ourselves, in our own might
For we have already gone through the darkest night
Yes, we have survived, we're still standing tall
Ever stronger, ready for any curveball

Life may throw us lemons and tears
But we'll handle it with grace and without any fears

For we know that nothing lasts forever
And we'll cherish each moment, be it good or whatever

So let's embrace the winds of change
And let our hearts and minds rearrange
For everything's uncertain, but that's okay
We'll face it all, every night and every day.

Sweet Part

All that you've been through is a constant reminder that there are things you cannot control. But the sweet part is that you have the ability to choose. With it, everything that is about to happen is worth everything. The struggles, frustrations, and pain you've been through are now history and that you've learned. This is the chapter where you will be rewarded for refusing to give up. Your choices get you through, and you continuously make the best version of yourself.

In life we face a constant reminder,
That things may happen beyond our control.
But in this chaos, there's a sweet glimmer,
Our ability to choose plays a vital role.

The struggles, frustrations, and all the pain,
Are mere chapters in the story we write.
For every loss, we have so much to gain,
With each choice, we pave the path so bright.

The past is gone, and now we stand,
Amidst the present, a blank canvas in hand.
We paint our future with each choice we make,
And every decision is a step we take.

The journey is long, but worth every stride,
For we're rewarded for refusing to give up.
Our choices get us through, and we take pride,
In making the best version of ourselves, no matter what

So let the history be a lesson learned,
And the present be the gift we embrace.
For the future is a blank page to be turned,
And we have the power to shape it with grace.

Spectrum of Emotions

The universe had your back; you're still standing and continue to do so. Every day you become aligned with your purpose and goals, which are learned through rough experiences. Now it doesn't bother you anymore; you've come to terms with welcoming the full spectrum of emotions. And to be okay, not to be okay.

In the vastness of the universe,
You stand tall, unyielding and strong,
The cosmos, like a shield, to disperse
All that might go against where you belong.

You've faced rough experiences and pain,
The kind that could have broken you down,
But the universe had your back, to sustain
Your spirit, to lift you up from the ground.

Every day, you align with your purpose,
With your goals, and with your dreams,
And as you journey, you never lose focus,
For the universe guides you with its beams.

With every step, you welcome the spectrum
Of emotions that come your way,

The highs and lows, the ups and downs,
For they've taught you how to live and stay.

Now you stand here, unafraid,
To be okay, not to be okay,
For the universe has your back, to aid
You, as you continue on your way.

And so, you move forward, with grace,
With the universe as your guide,
For you know that as you run this race,
You will always stand, side by side.

World of Uncertainty

On every page turned, there are twists and redirections of instances to spice up the story; the same is true with your life. A chapter has gone over with. Nonetheless, a new chapter begins. Start with a clean slate; begin with doubt, pain, and fear. It does not matter as long as you start now. Have faith in what you're becoming, for everything is possible in the world of uncertainty.

On every page turned, a tale unfolds,
With twists and turns, and secrets untold,
Every instance spiced up, with redirections abound,
A story so complex, its mysteries profound.

And just like a book, your life too,
Has chapters that end, and ones that are new,
A chapter now gone, with its lessons taught,
A new one awaits, with a clean slate brought.

Begin with doubt, and pain, and fear,
For they pave the way, for growth to appear,
It matters not how you begin, but when,
For every step forward, is a step towards the end.

Have faith in what you're becoming, my friend,
In this world of uncertainty, all things can bend,

The impossible is possible, if you just believe,
And hold onto hope, as you strive to achieve.

To turn the page, and start anew,
With each chapter, a different you,
Embrace the twists, and redirections of fate,
For they will lead you, to your destined state.

The Norm

Everyone seeks happiness. It seems looking for it is the norm, and you get upset if your expectations are not in your favor. Be patient; everything has its course. When your mind is clear, and you're in a good mood. Everything follows; you can thrive with all the upheavals on your way. Choose to move forward and move on positively. Give your best today, and tomorrow you'll be better.

In search of happiness, we all embark
A journey that seems forever dark
Expectations high, emotions at stake
Frustration looms if joy we cannot make

Patience, my friend, is what we need
For everything follows a destined lead
A clear mind and a joyful heart
Can help us soar, and never fall apart

The trials we face, the hardships we bear
Are mere obstacles, we mustn't despair
With a positive outlook, we can move ahead
And rise above, no matter what's said

For today's efforts, we must give our best
And tomorrow, we'll surpass the rest
With each new day, we can thrive
And happiness, we'll finally arrive.

Missing Out

Finding yourself stuck in the same routine and feeling frustrated? Don't be afraid of missing out; rather, be afraid of being in the same situation you are in now after one, five, or ten years. The struggle is real. You can find and focus on the things you love and begin there. This would make meaning in your life. Do it every day, then by doing so, you will wake up with the life you have created for yourself.

Tangled in the web of routine,
Feeling trapped, feeling obscene,
A mundane life, a constant scene,
Where dreams are lost, and hope unseen.

The struggle is real, it's true,
A fear of what the future will ensue,
To be stuck in the same old queue,
A life of nothingness, no breakthrough.

But fret not, my dear friend,
For there's light at the end,
In the things you love, time to spend,
A new beginning, a chance to amend.

Find your passion, and seize the day,
Make it your own, don't delay,
For every effort, there's a way,
To a brighter future, come what may.

Make it a habit, do it every day,
Live your life, don't just stay,
And soon you'll find, come what may,
Your dreams coming true, no more dismay.

Wake up to the life you've created,
A life of purpose, no longer jaded,
A heart full of love, no longer faded,
A life well-lived, no longer grated.

So take the first step, don't be shy,
And watch your life, as it takes flight,
For it's never too late to try,
And create a life, that's a delight.

Choose Your Hard

Doing nothing because you think you might be making a mistake. It is easy to stay in your comfort zone, expecting nothing to mess up. However, expect that there is also no room for growth and development. You know that everything complicated. Being motivated is hard, and staying broke is hard. Being single is complex, and being in a marriage is difficult. There is a reward in one pain and regret in another. You know yourself; you can do better. So, choose your hard.

In the comfort of our own thoughts,
We often find ourselves caught,
In the fear of taking a chance,
And making a mistake by circumstance.

It's easy to do nothing at all,
To avoid the risk of a fall,
But in doing so, we stagnate,
And leave ourselves to our own fate.

For growth and development to occur,
We must step out of our comfort blur,
And face the challenges that lie ahead,
With courage and resilience instead

We know that everything is hard,
Being motivated can leave us scarred,
Staying broke can be a constant pain,
Being single or married can drive us insane.

But in these struggles, there is a reward,
And inaction, there is regret to afford,
We know ourselves, we can do better,
So, choose your hard, and be a go-getter.

The road to success is never easy,
But it's worth it, believe me,
For every step forward, we gain,
New skills, knowledge, and strength to obtain.

So, don't let the fear of mistakes hold you back,
Take a chance, and stay on track,
For in the end, the reward is grand,
And you'll be proud of where you stand.

Backup Plan

Daily habits can play a significant role in change. Whom you share your energy with and the people surrounding you can impact you. How you speak to yourself and the kind of book you read validate who you are. You are a work in progress, and it's getting better each time. Be kind to yourself just as you treat your best friend. Yourself is the only backup plan; be sure you got your back.

Daily habits, a simple way to start,
But can play a big role in change, impart
Small changes, every day, can make a difference
And transform your life, with persistence

Whom you share your energy with, it's true
Can impact you, like a domino effect, who knew
Surrounding yourself with positivity and light
Can make your journey, a lot more bright

How you speak to yourself, with kindness and care
Can make you feel better, and take you somewhere
Validation, from the kind of book you read
Can impact your beliefs, and inspire lead

You are a work in progress, every day
Don't give up, keep striving, in every way

It's getting better each time, never forget
You are capable of achieving, the highest of the set

Be kind to yourself, just like your best friend
Encourage and uplift, to the very end
Yourself is the only backup plan, that's true
Be sure you got your back, in everything you do

So take a step, and start with a habit today
Small changes, can lead to a better way
Remember, you are in charge, of your destiny
And with every habit, you can set yourself free.

Celebrate Yourself

Always choose yourself and keep striving for good. Not everybody has a heart like yours; the worst is that they might have different intentions that might crumble what you've worked hard for. Consider being the best version of yourself. You're beautiful as it is and might not be everyone's cup of tea; nevertheless, you are a unique character. You've been through a lot that made you who you are now. Celebrate yourself, for you are one of a kind.

In the midst of life's great change,
Daily habits hold the key,
To the progress we attain,
And the person we will be.

The people that we surround
Are like seeds that we will sow,
Energy we share around
Will make our progress grow.

The way we speak, and the words we choose,
Shape the person that we are,
The books we read, the thoughts we muse,
Validate our inner star.

We are works of art in progress,
Flesh and bone and heart and mind,
Every day, we must confess,
We are getting better, refined

Be kind to yourself each day,
As you would to your best friend,
For yourself is the only way,
To make progress to the end.

And when the road ahead seems bleak,
And your hope begins to lack,
Remember, you are not weak,
For you've got your own back.

Two

It's okay to be scared, for you are bigger than your fear.

Rollercoaster

Overthinking sometimes gets you on a rollercoaster of emotions which causes you to carry a spiral of troubles. Do realize that things turn out better than you imagined; it tends to end up working out. It's hard to believe what you can't see; don't underestimate yourself. See the bigger picture and believe where you're heading. Nobody can do it better than you.

Overthinking, a treacherous path to tread,
A rollercoaster ride of emotions in your head,
A spiral of troubles, a weight that you bear,
A journey that leads you to nowhere.

But do not despair, my friend, for there is hope,
For things turn out better than you can cope,
The universe has its way, its path to unfold,
A story that's yet to be told.

So do not underestimate yourself, my dear,
Believe in your worth, do not fear,

See the bigger picture, the grand design,
The destination that's yours, it's simply divine.

Trust in the journey, and enjoy the ride,
For nobody can do it better than you, don't hide,
Embrace the ups and downs, the twists and turns,
For it's the journey that teaches us, not the outcomes we yearn.

Overthinking can be a tough habit to break,
But with each passing day, take a step, don't hesitate,
Believe in yourself, and trust in your heart,
For your journey is unique, it's your own work of art.

So let's bid farewell to the rollercoaster ride,
And embrace the path that's meant for you to stride,
A journey of discovery, of learning, and growth,
For nobody can do it better than you, my friend, boast!

Make It Count

It is time to start accommodating yourself more than others. You've been betrayed and abused, and you've tried. It seems not working much for you. Stop being the person you think everyone else wants you to be. Work on how you want to be, the best version of yourself. Those who value you for who you are will stick around. You only have one life, be sure to make it count.

In life we often find ourselves
Trying to please those around us
We mold ourselves into what they want
Without even realizing the fuss

We sacrifice our own desires
To fit into their mold
But in the end, we're left exhausted
Our hearts and minds feeling cold

We've been betrayed and abused
But we still try to please
Thinking it's the only way
To put our troubled hearts at ease

But it's time to make a change
To start accommodating ourselves

To work on being the best version
Of who we are, and nothing else

We'll find that those who truly care
Will stick around through thick and thin
They'll accept us for who we are
And see the light that shines within

We only have one life to live
So let's make it count, it's true
By valuing ourselves and our worth
We'll become the best version of me and you.

Tick Away

Every day is not the same, some days are good, and some days you wish it to be over. But time doesn't stop when it is not convenient. Clocks tick away, and the sun continues to move west. So, when you're having a great time, savor the moment and keep the memories in your heart. When bad days return, keep your cool and believe they will pass. You're capable and have the wisdom to go through the chaos. This is just a hump in your way. Keep going.

Every day, we wake up to the sun,
With hopes and dreams, we continue on to run.
Some days are filled with joy and laughter,
While some leave us feeling broken and shattered.

The clock keeps ticking, time never waits,
We go through life with different fates.
The sun moves west, the day turns to night,
Minutes turn to hours, and time takes flight.

On great days, we bask in the glory,
Memories made, they're part of our story.
We savor the moment, cherish the past,
Hoping these good times would forever last.

But on bad days, we feel the weight,
Heavy burdens, we try to escape.
We keep our cool, hold our heads high,
Knowing deep down we will get by.

For we are capable, we have the strength,
To go through the chaos, no matter the length.
With wisdom gained from past struggles,
We face the challenges without any troubles.

Every day is not the same,
Some days bring fortune, and some bring pain.
But we keep going, fighting each hump,
Knowing that we can overcome.

It's Okay

There are reasons why you do the things you do. It could be that previously you gained knowledge and joy from it. And some instances that you now avoid because of frustrations and heartbreaks. However, there is the thing that scares you, and it's okay. If you think it would do you good, go for it. You are bigger than your fear; moreover, you are in a position to be brave. Go ahead, be scared, and do it anyway. A beautiful future awaits.

Within the confines of my mind,
A million thoughts I seek to find,
The reasons why I do the things I do,
And why some paths I now eschew.

Perhaps a joy it brought before,
Or knowledge gained, an open door,
But heartbreak and frustration now,
Have left me wary, I avow.

Yet there's a thing that scares me so,
A fear that grips and won't let go,
But if it holds the promise bright,
Of good to come, of future light.

Then I must be brave and take the chance,
To step forward, despite this dance,

Of fear and doubt within my head,
To face the unknown, where paths may tread.

For I am more than any fear,
And stronger still, when I draw near,
To what I fear, to what I dread,
And face it boldly, without dread.

So go ahead, be scared, it's fine,
But take that step, cross the line,
To where a beautiful future waits,
Where dreams and hopes, at last, conflate.

Unapologetically You

When you wake up in the morning, you get a chance to be different and change. You know now what makes you tick to be productive for yourself. Use your energy to make other's life, particularly your life, meaningful and extraordinary. Your past is now history; take the good from the bad and start from there. Your actions determine whom you'll become tomorrow. Be unapologetically you.

When the sun rises in the morn,
A new chance to be reborn,
To shake off the weight of yesterday,
And pave the path for a brighter way.

The ticking clock reminds us so,
That time is fleeting, it won't slow,
We must seize the day with fervor,
And make each moment full of ardor.

Our energy is a precious gift,
To use it well, our spirits lift,
We can make a difference in others' lives,
And shape the world in which we thrive.

But let us not forget ourselves,
For happiness and meaning lie on these shelves,
We must be true to who we are,
And from our own light, we'll see afar.

Our past may bring regret and pain,
But we can use it to our gain,
Take the lessons learned and move ahead,
And from the ashes, new life is bred.

Our actions now will pave the way,
For who we'll be tomorrow and each new day,
So let us not hold back or fear,
But be unapologetically sincere.

For in the end, it's not the fame,
Or fortune that will bring us acclaim,
But living a life that's true and pure,
And leaving behind a legacy that endures.

Your Shine

Now is the time to forgive yourself for what you've accepted. Frustrations, heartaches, and manipulations are now out of the table. You gave the best part of yourself and were taken for granted; you know you just wanted to be loved in the right way. It's time to be selfish and care for yourself first. Don't let your heart become bitter; you're beautiful and strong. You've endured and conquered. Bring out your shine; you've got this.

In the depths of anguish and despair,
When love seemed distant and rare,
You gave your heart with all your might,
Hoping it would shine in the light.

But time and again, it was taken for granted,
Your trust and love, left stranded,
Frustrations, heartaches, and manipulations,
Were the only things left in your relations.

Now is the time to forgive yourself,
For what you've accepted, put on the shelf,
The pain and hurt, let them go,
And let your heart begin to glow.

Be selfish and care for yourself first,
Let your needs and desires finally burst,
Don't let your heart become bitter,
You're beautiful and strong, don't let them litter.

You've endured and conquered with all your might,
You've fought through the darkest of night,
It's time to bring out your shine,
And let your spirit soar and shine.

So rise above the doubts and fears,
Let your light shine through the tears,
Now is the time to forgive and move on,
And let your heart rejoice in a brand new dawn.

For you've got this; you're strong and true,
And with each step, you'll find the path anew,
So go ahead and take that leap,
And let your spirit soar, high and deep.

Inner Depths

It is okay because this time, you'll fight for yourself. You've realized you're tired of being a puppet or a clown; enough is enough. They were just not the right person for you to give your energy to in the first place. Focus on what is worth it all along, so it is okay. Today, you will do what your passion is. Follow what you enjoy and have an interest in. Explore the inner depths of your soul, for you are worth every smile, appreciation, and attention. You are loved.

Amidst the chaos and the noise,
You stood there, feeling quite coy.
Tired of being a puppet or a clown,
You decided to rise, to stand your ground.

Gave your energy to the wrong ones,
Squandered your time like the setting sun.
But now you know, you've realized,
That it's okay to fight for your own prize.

You focus on what is worth it all,
Follow your passion and hear your call.
Explore your soul's innermost depths,
And find what brings you boundless breadth.

For you are worth every smile,
Every appreciation, every attention worthwhile.
Today, with renewed vigor and zeal,
You march forth towards something real.

No more living life on someone's terms,
No more entertaining their frivolous whims.
You are worth more than that, my dear,
Your worth shines bright and clear.

So let the world watch as you rise,
As you set your sights on the skies.
Be proud, for you are loved and adored,
And your journey has only just begun to soar.

Preparation

True, you have to go through hurdles life throws at you. You can't screw, but you can rest if you think it's getting heavier. It's confusing how things work with others and not with you. Remind yourself that you have your own time. It might be a bit late ad seems nothing is happening, but if you look back, you can see how far you've come. Continue and push through, one day at a time. The door will continue to open for those who persevere; waiting is not punishment but preparation.

Life is a maze of hurdles to surmount,
A course to navigate, and not just count,
A journey that tests our every skill,
And beckons us to climb another hill.

But, when the load seems too much to bear,
It's not time to give up, but to take a break and repair,
For rest is not a sign of weakness or defeat,
But a chance to recharge and get back on your feet.

It's easy to compare our lives with those of others,
To feel frustrated and lost when things don't fall into place
like feathers,

But, we must remember that our lives are unique,
And time will unfold at its own flick.

Sometimes, it may seem that we're stuck in a rut,
And our efforts aren't going anywhere, but remember to not
stay put,
For if you look back, you'll see how far you've come,
And how much you've achieved since you've begun.

It's true that the journey may be long and tough,
And the road ahead may seem rough,
But with each step, you gain momentum and strength,
And inch closer to your dream at any length.

So, continue to push through, one day at a time,
And never give up, even when the climb seems like a crime,
For the door will open for those who persevere,
And waiting is not a punishment, but preparation for the
grand premiere.

Underrated

The feeling to belong in the wrong people can be exhausting. You've tried not being who you are and walking on eggshells just to fit in. It doesn't feel good. Taming yourself and lowering your lights is not helping at all. Why not stop being underrated and choose to be the real you? Stop being surrounded by poor treatment and radical judgment. You are better alone, and you can find people who can understand your quirkiness and would accept them. Let it out. You're unique in your own way. The world made you for a reason.

In a world full of noise and chaos,
Where we strive to fit in and belong,
It's easy to lose ourselves in the process,
And feel like we don't belong.

We try to be who we're not,
Walking on eggshells, taming ourselves,
In a bid to fit in with the crowd,
But it only leaves us feeling exhausted.

We feel underrated, unseen,
As we dim our lights and hide our quirks,
In a desperate attempt to be accepted,
But it only leads to radical judgmen

It's time to stop and embrace who we are,
To let our true selves shine through,
For we are unique in our own way,
And the world needs our light too.

It's not about fitting in,
But finding those who understand,
Who accept us for who we are,
And lift us up to greater heights.

So let go of the need to please,
And be who you were meant to be,
For in the end, it's not about the crowd,
But about the person you were made to be.

Decision

The decision to let a person go is not easy, especially if a space in your heart is already attached. It could be a relief and gain back joy if the relationship brings more misery than positivity. It could be the toughest decision; you may feel like it can break you at a certain point. However, have faith that this will bring you back to the life you want, not the life that someone is forcing you to have.

The Decision to Let Go

The path of love is seldom straight,
It winds and curves with twists of fate,
And oftentimes we find our heart,
Attached to one who's torn us apart.

The joy we once held in our soul,
Is swallowed up by pain and toll,
And though we try to make it right,
We find ourselves in endless fights.

The space within our heart is filled,
With someone who has left us chilled,
And though we know we should let go,
We hold on tight and fight the flow.

The decision to let a person go,
Is not an easy one to know,
For though we long to be set free,
We fear what life without them will be.

The toughest choice we'll ever make,
Is to release our heart's mistake,
And though it feels like we'll break down,
We must have faith in what is found.

For in the end, when we let go,
We open up a brand new flow,
And life will bring us back to light,
Free from the misery and the fight.

So though the tears may flood our eyes,
And though we feel we'll never rise,
We must have faith that we will find,
The life we want, the peace of mind.

Post Traumatic Growth

When you look back on the past years, don't think of the difficulties you've gone through. You turned your back on them, and these were the fights you won. You know you didn't stay for a particular reason. Instead, think of how you came this far and the post-traumatic growth it caused you, let alone the strength you've gained. You are becoming the ideal person you've wanted to be, which is liberating. Respect and give yourself credit for your courage and resilience. Your beautiful life awaits. Proceed with grace.

Gazing into the past, you see a path
Wrought with difficulties, trials amassed
But don't focus on the struggles you've faced
Instead, turn your back and see how you've aced

Each fight you've conquered is a victory won
Each obstacle overcome, a battle done
You didn't stay for a reason, now it's clear
You're becoming the person you always held dear

Post-traumatic growth, a strength you've gained
From the trials you faced, the pain sustained
It wasn't easy, but you persevered
With courage and resilience, you've steere

Towards a life that's beautiful and bright
One that's filled with hope and delight
Respect yourself for how far you've come
And give yourself the credit you've won

For the grace with which you proceed
Towards a future that's yours to lead
Your journey is your own, unique and true
And the person you're becoming is all because of you.

Unpeeled Layers

Day to day, you find it ordinary and sometimes dull. People around you get on your nerve sometimes. You feel like there's nothing ever new that is going to happen. Brace yourself; those days were honing you to bring out the unpeeled layers of your being. It has reached your soul; you don't realize how amazing you are. All of what you've worked for was worth it. You are blessed and claim you're on your way to a wonderful life.

Day to day, mundane and routine
The world around you, an endless scene
People and their quirks, getting on your nerve
Leaving you feeling, it's all so absurd

Nothing new, nothing exciting
Life seems to lack, any inviting
But hold on tight, for these days prepare
Honing you, for the greatness you'll wear

Unpeeling the layers, of your being
Revealing the inner strength, you're freeing
It reaches your soul, in ways untold
Only then, the beauty of life unfolds

You are amazing, beyond measure
Your worth, cannot be simply treasured
All you've worked for, was worth the strife
Leading you, to a blessed life

So embrace the mundane, with open arms
For it's the catalyst, to your charms
You're on your way, to a life so fine
Filled with joy, and purpose divine.

The Act

Time passes by, depending on what you're doing. Don't compare yourself to others' success or accomplishments. You're not late or behind as long as you have started or are yet to start. Don't listen to people who've nothing to add to your value. The secret is to act and be consistent. Anything is possible, and you have all that it takes. Dream big, and start small, but the most important is to start and give your all.

In the endless expanse of time,
A clock ticks on, a rhythm sublime,
Each second, minute, hour that goes by,
A reminder that life, too, will fly.

But fret not if you're yet to start,
Or if you're taking a different part,
For comparison is a fickle game,
And the rules are never quite the same.

Your journey, your story, your pace,
Is unique to you, a one-of-a-kind race,
So don't be fooled by others' success,
Or their accomplishments, their progress.

Those who offer naught but noise,
Are merely empty, shallow toys,
Their words a burden, a weight to bear,
As they try to dim your dreams, your flair.

But the secret lies in action, in deed,
In the courage to start and to proceed,
To stay the course, to be consistent, true,
And to yourself, always remain faithful too.

With all that it takes, within your grasp,
Anything is possible, no task too vast,
Dream big, aim high, look towards the sky,
But know that to take flight, you must first try.

So take that first step, however small,
And let your heart lead, your spirit call,
For in the end, what matters most,
Is not the speed, but the journey, the host.

Time passes by, but fear not the tide,
For in your heart, you have all you need inside,
To make your dreams come true, to give your all,
And to rise, like a phoenix, from the ashes of any fall.

Stitches

You often beat yourself because of the things that turned messy that you don't have control over. Relax, feel the pain to heal. It's an unconventional art that gets you through the unbearable and is where strength is developed. Be patient with yourself, and slowly recover from the stitches you made to get yourself back together. It wouldn't be easy, but you'll endure and get through. Nevertheless, you are worth the struggle. Breathe, you got this.

In moments of despair, you may feel undone,
By things that turned messy, beyond your control,
You beat yourself up, for the battles not won,
And let your pain consume, your heart and soul.

But hold on tight, and don't let go,
For there's an art to healing that you should know,
It's unconventional, yet effective, they say,
And helps you bear the unbearable, every day.

It asks you to relax, and feel the pain,
Embrace the struggle, and dance in the rain,
For through the storm, you learn to grow,
And strength is developed, within your soul.

Be patient with yourself, and take it slow,
Recover from the stitches, you made to glow,
It may not be easy, but you'll endure and fight,
For you are worth the struggle, and the journey's light.

So breathe in deep, and let it out,
You got this, there's no need to doubt,
The path may be rocky, and the road may be tough,
But you'll emerge a warrior, and that's enough.

Boundaries

Life itself consumes you with everything happening, worst if it's not in your favor. Baby steps and one day at a time are essential to survival, and with these processes of going through challenging times, you've learned the most lesson. I'm proud of you; now you have your boundaries not to keep people out but to ensure that only the right ones can come in. Experiences make you wiser and know now that not because someone is nice would be good for you, or they will treat you the way you want to be treated.

In life's unending cycle, we're consumed
With all that happens, as fate is entombed
And if the stars don't align in our favor
Our world crumbles, and we lose our flavor

But baby steps, one day at a time
Are the keys to survival, and we must climb
Through the valleys of hardship and strife
To reach the summit, and embrace new life

For it is in the darkness we learn the most
And with each challenge, we become engrossed
In the lessons that come with our struggles
And the knowledge that makes our minds juggle

So be proud of yourself, for you have grown
And established boundaries, to call your own
Not to keep people out, but to ensure
That only the right ones walk through your door

For experiences make us wise beyond measure
And we know now, that not all that's pleasurable
Is good for us, or will treat us as we deserve
And that not all who seem nice, can preserve

The sanctity of our souls, and our inner peace
So we must be careful, and not just appease
But choose those who add value to our lives
And let go of those who bring only strife

Life is a journey, with twists and turns
But with each lesson, our spirit burns
Brighter and stronger, with wisdom and grace
And we emerge victorious, in every race.

Refined Version

Being strong for so long can make you tired, and you would like to give up. Don't you dare; you can rest if you must but believe that you've been molded to be a refined version of yourself. Your strength and courage will take you a long way though underrated sometimes. Do remember that you've come a long way; continue to help yourself. Believe that you are strong to go through obstacles in life and fight for the future you've always wanted.

With every stride you take,
A step closer to your fate, T
he journey's long, the road is rough,
The climb is steep, and the going's tough.

Being strong for so long, it seems,
Can drain you of your strength and dreams,
But don't give up, don't let it go,
Take a break, rest, and keep the flow.

Believe that you've been shaped and molded,
Into a refined version of yourself, unfolded,
Your strength and courage, though underrated,
Will take you far, even when you're faded.

You've come a long way, don't forget,
The battles won, the tears you've shed,
Keep helping yourself, never give in,
For you are strong, and the fight you'll win.

Obstacles will come, that's for sure,
Challenges will arise, and you'll endure,
But believe that you have what it takes,
To fight for the future your heart makes.

So when you're tired, and you feel weak,
Remember, you're not alone, and you can seek,
The strength within, the courage to fight,
For the future that shines so bright.

So take a breath, and keep pushing through,
The journey's long, but you'll make it too,
For you are strong, and you've got this in you,
Just keep going, and your dreams will come true.

Know You

Start with yourself; no better person can know you more than you do. You know when you feel cared for and treated poorly, so don't let others tell you what is good for you. Rely on your senses and gut feeling, and you won't miss. You are good enough to love yourself even if others don't see it that way. Forcing others to see your value is worthless, they will find reasons to criticize and gaslight the reality. Be brave to be alone on your walks and dinners and go through the night. Above all, every little success of yours is worth a celebration.

Within yourself, you'll find the key
To living life both bold and free
For no one knows you quite like you
Your thoughts and feelings, pure and true

Don't let others dictate your fate
Or tell you what is good or great
Your senses and your gut will lead
To choices that you truly need

You're good enough just as you are
No need to change or go too far

Don't force others to see your worth
Or let them drag you down to earth

Embrace your solitude with pride
And take those lonely walks outside
Enjoy your dinners on your own
And revel in the silence grown

Each little win deserves a cheer
No matter how small, it's clear
So celebrate your victories
And hask in life's sweet mysteries

For in yourself, you'll find the way
To live a life both bright and gay
So trust in you and all you do
And watch your dreams come into view.

A Warrior

You used to be somebody else, a pleasing, timid, innocent, and agreeable person. Then turned out to be people you loved most, let you down, broke your heart, and treated you inadequately. Such a hard pill to swallow that struck you with the reality that no matter how good you are, you will never be good enough for the wrong person. Put yourself back together; for now, you're more able to handle pain, misery, and frustration. You've turned out to be somebody you would never think you would. It takes an amount of strength, and you've chosen yourself. You're incredibly strong. You're a warrior.

Once upon a time, you were someone else
Pleasing, timid, innocent, agreeable, nothing else
People loved you, adored you, you were their pride
But their love was transient, withered away and died

The ones you held closest, shattered your heart
Their inadequacy, a hard pill to swallow, tore you apart
You realized that no matter how good you are
For the wrong person, it's never enough, they leave a scar

But you picked up the pieces, put yourself back together
For pain, misery, and frustration, you're now tougher than
leather
You turned out to be someone you never thought you would be
A warrior, strong and resilient, that's what you are, can't you
see?

It takes an immense amount of strength to rise from the ashes
The journey's tough, but the destination's worth the lashes
You've chosen yourself, and that's the best decision you've
made
The road's not easy, but hey, you're a warrior, you're unafraid

Now you know that being good enough for the wrong person's
a myth
The truth is, you're enough, don't ever let anyone tell you
otherwise with a pith
You've come a long way, learned from your struggles, and pain
You're more than what they thought, you're a warrior, you're
insane!

So embrace the change, welcome the new you
You're strong, resilient, and that's what you should pursue
Keep moving forward, and never look back
Because, my dear warrior, your future's bright, that's a fact.

Right to Live

With all that you have to deal with, your choices and decisions ultimately direct you in what your goals are. Be mindful not to be persuaded by what others want you to be. You know yourself better than anyone else; you have the right to live your chosen life. It comes with where your heart's happiness is and what would make you tick. If you're not yet there, don't lose hope. It's just around the corner, and better things are always ahead. Believe that you're stronger than any upheavals that come your way. You are exactly where you are meant to be now and in the direction you're heading. It takes time for beautiful things to happen.

Amidst the trials and tribulations of life,
Your choices and decisions pave the way
Towards the goals you seek, through toil and strife,
And lead you closer to the light of day.

Be mindful not to let the world decide
What path you take, what person you become,
For only you can know what's deep inside
And where your heart's true happiness is from.

*If you're not there just yet, don't lose your hope, For better
things are waiting to appear,*

*Like rainbows after storms that help us cope,
And beauty after hardship brings us cheer.*

*Believe that you are stronger than the waves
That crash and toss you on the ocean's tide,
For deep within you lies the strength that saves
And keeps you moving forward with great pride.*

*You are exactly where you're meant to be,
In the direction of your chosen fate,
And though it's hard to wait and simply see,
It takes time for beautiful things to date.*

*So hold your head up high and take a breath,
For every step you take is one more close
To where your heart's true happiness is left,
And every hardship conquered is a boast.*

*With all that you have to deal with, know this,
Your choices and decisions are your own,
And when you follow your heart's true bliss,
The beauty of your life will surely shown.*

A Fighter

You've been the giver most of the time. Your time, energy, effort, and most of all, your love. Where did it go? Down the drain, blown out of the window, or gone and forgotten. Now you've realized that you can't force yourself to receive back what you do for others. Start giving yourself the same amount of good stuff and watch it thrive. This time you'll not get hurt and frustrated, for you know what to expect in return. From all of where you're coming from, you'll become the best version of yourself, happy and contented, without the help of anyone. A fighter lives within you. You're incredible.

You've given much, with love and care
Time, effort, energy to spare
But where did it all disappear?
Down the drain, gone without a tear?

You can't force others to reciprocate
To give back what you've done so great
It's time to focus on yourself
To create a life of joy and wealth

Start giving yourself the same amount
Of love and care, without a doubt

Watch as your life begins to thrive
No longer feeling hurt or deprived

From where you've been, you'll rise above
The best version of yourself, filled with love
A fighter lives within your soul
You're incredible, you'll reach your goal

Now go forth, and shine so bright
Your future is filled with light
No longer needing anyone's aid
You're happy and content, you've got it made.

Valid

Taking in so much at a time sometimes is exhausting. You wish that sometimes you could feel numb to calm everything down for a bit. Relax and have a peaceful mind, not wondering what could happen differently and what if you'd done it the other way. Overthinking could hold you back; let go and let it fold how it should be. Accept that whatever you feel is valid; moreover, there are reasons why you feel every single of them. It must even be stupid to have certain emotions at times, but they are relevant to who you are. So, don't apologize; I assure you that all your emotions are valid. You matter.

Taking in so much at a time,
Can leave you feeling spent and tired,
Wishing for numbness to calm the mind,
And ease the rush that leaves you wired.

Relaxing is the key to peace,
A moment to just let it be,
Stop wondering what could've been,
And let the future unfold naturally.

Overthinking can be a hindrance,
Holding you back from what could be,

But let go, it'll all make sense,
Just trust that it's meant to be.

All emotions are valid,
Even if they seem absurd,
It's okay to feel what you feel,
For emotions are part of the world.

There's no need to apologize,
For being true to who you are,
For all your emotions are valid,
And they matter, by far.

Through It All

There was a time that you wanted to say so much, lots going in your head that you wanted to get it out. Nevertheless, you fought yourself back and rather said so little. Thinking it's easier to avoid disagreement than to challenge what you believe in is not a big deal. You felt so much that you felt you'd explode if you let it lose. However, you kept yourself in control and instead stayed so silent. You wished that it would soon be over and get through it all.

There was a time, not long ago,
When words inside would ebb and flow,
A torrential storm of thoughts and fears,
That threatened to break hopes and tears.

So much to say, so much to share,
A burden heavy, hard to bear,
And yet, you chose to hold it in,
To bottle up your thoughts within.

Perhaps you feared the world outside,
Or maybe silence felt your only guide,
For standing up and making noise,
Could lead to strife, could kill your joys.

It's true, disagreement can be tough,
A challenge, a fight, a road that's rough,
But living in a world that's grey,
Is worse than holding fears at bay.

You felt it all, the pain, the hurt,
The anger that could make you burst,
And yet, you kept it all inside,
Your heart and soul, you chose to hide.

It's hard to keep control, to stay composed,
When chaos reigns, and peace is prone to erode,
But you, my friend, you did it well,
You fought the war within yourself.

And though it felt like time stood still,
And every day felt like a test of will,
You held on tight, you kept your ground,
And soon enough, you came around.

The storm may rage, the winds may blow,
But deep within, you'll always know,
That bravery lies not in the sword,
But in the choice to speak your word.

So hold your head up high, my friend,
And let your voice be heard again,
For though the road may twist and bend,
Your courage will not see its end.

Yourself

You've been patiently playing your part. Thus, one day, you'll wake up and decide for a change. You can't continue any longer. You've given all, and you're drained. You left nothing for yourself but bruises and scars of pain. It's not over; it is now the time to take care of yourself, just like how you took care of others. Because at the end of the day, you can only rely on yourself. Accept that you're a high-value person, and no one can say any less.

You've been the strongest of them all,
Patiently playing your part on call,
Lending a hand without any doubt,
Never minding the cost nor the clout.

Days and nights, you've been there,
For every soul that needed care,
Your heart aches, but you persist,
For the ones you love, you insist.

But one day, a realization dawns,
You can't go on with the same old songs,
You're drained, exhausted, and worn,
Bruises and scars, you're left to mourn.

It's not over, it's time for change,
For you to break free from this range, T
o take care, to nurture your own,
To heal the wounds, to calm the groans.

For at the end of the day, it's you,
Who can rely on, who can pull through,
You're a high-value person, it's true,
And nothing can take that away from you.

So don't let anyone say any less,
You deserve happiness and success,
It's time for you to shine and bloom, To
break free from the gloom and doom.

You've given your all, now it's time,
To stand tall, to be sublime,
To embrace the joy, to seize the day,
To be the one who leads the way.

So go ahead, take the reins,
Take control, break the chains,
Live your life, be true to yourself,
For you're worth more than anyone else.

Three

Even if you're vulnerable, you're always there.
But you also deserve the same in return.

Limitless

Your thoughts are powerful, and they can turn into reality. It is limitless to what you can imagine with no boundaries. Guard your thoughts, translate your thinking into small steps, and act on them. Do your chosen plan on how to go with your goal. It is impossible to get worse at something you do each day consistently. Everything will eventually unfold. Furthermore, you will reap what you planted. Trust yourself in the process; no one says it's going to be easy, and it cannot be done overnight. But you got all that it takes; you've been through hell and back. What else is there to be scared of? Take a deep breath and take your path. You've got this.

Deep within your mind lies the key
To unlock the doors of possibility

Your thoughts are like seeds in soil
Plant them well, and they'll unfurl

With no limits to what you can conceive
Visualize and believe, don't deceive
For thoughts transform into reality
With power, you can't ignore or flee

Guard them well, these precious gems
And translate them into small steps
Act on them with unwavering faith
And the world will follow your pace

Choose your path and make a plan
Each day, do something to advance
Consistency is the key to success
Even a little progress becomes progress

The road may be long, winding, and rough
But with perseverance, you will triumph
Trust the process, and never give up
The fruits of your labor will fill your cup

You are capable of achieving great things
Even when the sky above you sings

Of doubt, fear, and uncertainty
Believe in yourself and your ability

You've been through fire and come out strong
What else is there to be scared of for long?
Take a deep breath and stand tall
Your journey is yours to make and control

Your thoughts are powerful, never forget
They shape your reality, they're not just a set
Of random musings or fleeting ideas
They're the foundation of all that you'll achieve.

Sanity

Values, yes, it is fundamental to a person. It shows how the level of dignity you're at and your boundaries are to safeguard your sanity. Having values isn't a threat though it's a source not everybody can reckon with. It is meant to stop the engagement to anyone's toxicity and only entertain one's purposeful intention. You've dealt with more than enough drama that causes you to be sorrowful. It's not your music to dance to let alone not your circus, not your monkeys. You've carried the load, and it was getting heavier each time.

Values, oh values, how they define,
The dignity we hold, the boundaries we align,
A safeguard for our sanity, a beacon to guide,
A source not everyone can reckon with, a pride.

It's not a threat, no, not at all,
It's a shield against toxicity's call,
To entertain the purposeful intention,
And stop engagement with malice's invention.

We've dealt with drama, oh yes we have,
The sorrowful tunes we couldn't bear to have,

It's not our music to dance to,
Nor our circus, nor our monkeys to shoe.

The load we've carried, oh it's been heavy,
Each time it grew, our strength unsteady,
But with values by our side,
We marched on, with hearts open wide.

For values, yes, they are fundamental,
To a person, to a community, to a nation so gentle,
We hold them dear, we cherish their power,
For they make us better, each and every hour.

Intuition Speaks

Spare yourself, take the burden off your shoulders be in tune and aligned with how you feel. When your intuition speaks, always listen. You prosper when you're emotionally composed; you bond with those with the same intensity and vibrations because they value you. That's when you know your soul is at peace.

> On the path of life we all must tread,
> With burdens on our shoulders, heavy as lead,
> But spare yourself and let them go,
> For peace of mind, you must know.
>
> Be in tune with how you feel,
> Let your intuition show what's real,
> For when it speaks, always listen,
> And your heart will never glisten.
>
> Prosperity comes when you're composed,
> Emotionally aligned, never disclosed,
> With those who share the same vibrations,
> Only then, will you find relations.
>
> When you bond with those who value you,
> Your soul will sing, and your heart will renew,

Peace and harmony will be your reward,
For listening to the voice of the Lord.

So spare yourself, take the burden off your shoulders,
And let your heart sing with emotions bolder,
For when your soul is at peace,
Life's journey will be a beautiful lease.

How Dreary

Heart pulsating for the one you love, the depth where you keep them in your heart says it all. Ever ready to catch them when they fall, ears to listen when they need to rant and care when they are vulnerable. Nonetheless, you can say thank you for not making an effort and not treating yourself right in return. The lump in your throat seems permanent, and the heaviness in your heart keeps persistent. How dreary? You minimize it, for you want it to work.

The depth where you keep them in your heart says it all.
Ever ready to catch them when they fall,
Ears to listen when they need to rant,
And care when they are vulnerable.

You pour your soul into them,
Giving them pieces of your heart to hold.
You want them to know that you are there,
That you will always be their stronghold.

But what of the thankless days,
When they take without giving back?
When you are left with a lump in your throat,
And a heart that feels under attack?

You try to minimize the pain,
For you want it to work so much.
But the heaviness in your heart persists,
A constant reminder of your love's clutch.

You wonder if it's worth it,
If love is meant to be this hard.
But your heart keeps pulsating,
For the one you hold in regard.

So you soldier on, through thick and thin,
Hoping that someday they will see.
That the love you have for them is pure,
And you just want them to be free.

What Matters

Please understand that rejection and being ignored are meant to show that your worth is more remarkable; no reciprocity is madness. Everything you're ready to give if they are not ready to receive is meaningless. Don't stay if they do not value your time as much as you do. Get back to the track they took you off. You're better off being by yourself. You nurture what really matters, and that's you.

In life, we seek acceptance and love,
But sometimes we're met with a shove,
The rejection stings, the pain is real,
But in those moments, we must reveal,

That our worth is greater than we know,
And being ignored is just a show,
Of those who don't see our true light,
And those who don't value our might.

We offer ourselves, our time and care,
But if they don't reciprocate, beware,
For everything we're ready to give,
Is meaningless if they don't want to receive.

We mustn't stay where we're not wanted,
Or our value becomes haunted,
Our time is precious, our worth immeasurable,
And if they don't see that, it's unacceptable.

We must get back to the track we were on,
And remember where we truly belong,
We're better off being by ourselves,
Nurturing what really matters, our own selves.

It's not madness to seek what we deserve,
And if they can't see that, it's their loss to preserve,
We'll continue to shine bright and true,
And find those who value us, just like you.

Inner Peace

Don't beat yourself up for the poor behavior of others. They treat others on how they treat themselves, that shows who they really are. Stay kind, but don't be manipulated and safeguard your inner peace than trying to get your point across to a narrow-minded individual. People can only meet you at the level they are familiar with and can only pour your cup at the level they are comfortable with. Let them; don't force anyone to reach a level that you understand no matter how much you want to.

Don't beat yourself up, dear one,
For the poor behavior of others.
Their actions are not your burden,
Don't let them smother.

They treat others as they treat themselves,
Their actions show who they truly are.
Stay kind and firm, protect your health,
And don't let them go too far.

Safeguard your inner peace,
Don't be manipulated by their charm.
They try to make you cease,
But don't let them do you harm.

People can only meet you at their level,
They pour your cup at what they're comfortable with.
Don't force them to reach a revel,
That you understand, no matter how much you wish.

Let them be, and let them grow,
Don't make them feel inadequate.
Don't be harsh, let kindness flow,
And let them see a better fate.

You are not responsible for their actions,
So don't beat yourself up.
Protect your own satisfaction,
And let them fill their own cup.

Stay kind, and stay true,
And let them see by example.
They will learn from you,
And their hearts will soon unscramble.

Vibration

You're worthy of attention and appreciation, for your heart is pure. Continue to rise and connect where your vibrations meet. Right people will arrive moreover, see you of your worth. Keep shining. You're beautiful.

In this world of chaos and confusion,
Where everyone seeks love and admiration,
You stand tall with your heart pure,
Radiating love, shining bright for sure.

Your worthy soul deserves all the attention,
As you continue to rise with your pure intention,
Connecting with the universe's vibration,
Drawing in the right people with your attraction.

Let the naysayers and doubters fade away,
For they cannot see your brilliance on display,
Hold your head high, keep shining like a star,
For you are beautiful, just the way you are.

The journey may be tough, and the road may be long,
But your pure heart will keep you feeling strong,
Believe in yourself, and you'll go far,
For you are worthy of all the love and admiration you desire.

So keep on shining, my dear friend,
Your light will guide you till the very end,
And when the right people come into view,
They'll appreciate you for the beautiful soul that's true.

It Made You

Who you are now is the product of all the experiences you have been through. You have come a great way to reach a change for a better you, despite the things you have done that you are not proud of, decisions that make you think sometimes you wish you could change. The things that broke you and put you to rock bottom could have made you cold-hearted. Nevertheless, you chose not to, and you do not have regrets because it made you better.

Who you are now is a product, that's clear
Of all the experiences that you've held dear
From the highs and lows you've had to bear
To the trials and tribulations of which you're aware

You've come a long way to reach this change
For a better you, a life rearranged
Despite the things you've done that you're not proud of
You've learned from them and have risen above

Decisions that make you wish to change
Things you wish could be rearranged
But it's all a part of life's grand design
To make you stronger, to make you shine

The things that broke you, that put you to rock bottom
Could have made you cold-hearted, left you forgotten
But you chose a path that led to growth
And now you stand tall, a testament to both

Your strength and resilience, your will to survive
And all the lessons that you've learned to thrive
You don't have regrets, for it made you better
And now you're a shining example, to the letter

Of who you are now, and who you'll always be
A product of your experiences, for all to see
So embrace your past, and all that it entails
For it's helped you become the person, that proudly prevails.

Incredible

You can choose how pain and heartache will shape you; it's easier to be angry and hostile than to be kind and pleasant however, you choose to be shaped and become someone you come to love. You've developed and grown to be the person you do want to be. The character says a lot about a person, and to be who you are right now is incredible.

Pain and heartache, two forces untamed,
Can shape you into what you're meant to be.
An easy path, in anger and disdain,
But kind and nice, a harder road to see.

The choice is yours, to let pain lead the way,
To be negative and bitter in your heart.
Or to stand strong, with kindness as your stay,
And let love guide you from the start.

For who you become, is shaped by your choice,
The person you grow to love or hate.
Character speaks, a resounding voice,
And you alone decide your own fate.

To be who you are, through all the pain,
Is an incredible feat to behold.

A person of worth, who's grown and gained,
A heart of gold that will never grow old.

So choose wisely, and let love be your guide,
Through all the heartaches and the strife.
For the person you become on this ride,
Is the one who will live on in life.

Rehabilitation

When you've given your all to a person who matters to you, the care, time, and effort, it is a good feeling because you're a giver. You've seen the potential of a nice person. Nevertheless, it doesn't mean that if a person is nice, they can be good to you, let alone force them to be. Time passes by, and the layers eventually peel off. Behold a new person standing in front of you whom you don't even recognize. You've been a rehabilitation all along.

When you've given your all,
To a person you care for,
It's a feeling that takes its toll,
Yet, it makes you want to give more.

You see the potential shining bright,
In this person you've come to know,
And you give your time and effort with all your might,
As you watch your relationship grow.

But nice is not always good,
And potential can be deceiving,
As time passes, the layers you understood,
Slowly start to unravel revealing.

A new person emerges,
One you don't even recognize,
And you're left to witness,
The harsh truth with open eyes.

You were the rehabilitation,
All along unaware,
Trying to fix and mend their situation,
But now you're left to bear.

The weight of disappointment and regret,
For pouring your heart and soul,
Into someone who could forget,
All the love and care you showed.

But don't let this experience break you,
For you're a giver at heart,
Learn and grow from what you've been through,
And let this be a fresh start.

You've given your all to someone who mattered,
But it's time to give to yourself,
For the layers that have been shattered,
Have left you with a story to tell.

So take a deep breath and let it out,
And know that you're not alone,
For there's a new day ahead, no doubt,
And you've still got love to be shown.

The Goal

This time, you have to give the space without the need to save, fix or even heal the person; rather, let them soak in their feeling. It's not your responsibility to change them. You've reached your limits and have to take care of yourself. It's not being selfish; putting yourself first to save your well-being is the goal. Your needs matter too.

In this moment, you stand so strong,
With knowledge that you must belong
To your own needs, your own desires,
To save yourself, to stoke your fires.

It's not your job to fix or mend
The broken souls who can't ascend
To where you stand, with steady ground,
With all the answers that you've found.

You've given all that you can give,
And now it's time to simply live
For you, for what you need and want,
To let your own heart take the front.

It's not an act of selfishness,
To put yourself in your own dress,
To wear your needs upon your sleeve,
To take the space that you believe

Is yours, and yours alone to claim,
To let others feel their own pain,
Without the need to intervene,
Or try to fix the things unseen.

You've reached your limits, that's okay,
It's time to heal, to find your way
To peace, to love, to happiness,
To put yourself in your own nest.

Through Days

Keep going though days are not always the same. It can be good and, at times, unbearable; as the saying goes, "When it rains, it pours." Though you've been hurt, heartbroken, and manipulated, you still stay on your ground, your head held high. You've picked up the strength to push through even though you knew it would have been easier to give up. Your courage takes you to a diffcrent level to overcome fear, better over bitter, productive over being cold, and choosing to be open to love and be love.

In this life, we all must learn,
To take a turn and let ourselves yearn,
For a gift of space and time,
To let our spirits truly shine.

We need to step away from the fray,
And not just fix or chase all day,
The broken pieces that we see,
But rather let ourselves be free.

Free to feel the weight of life,
To soak it in, to feel the strife,
And let our souls take a deep breath,
To find the courage to confront death.

Towards the sky, towards the light,
We need to find our own true fight,
For all the things that make us whole,
For all the things that make us bold.

Sometimes we need to break away,
From all the curves that lead astray,
And find the peace that we've been seeking,
To live the life that we've been dreaming.

So take the space that you deserve,
And let yourself just freely curve,
Into the mold that you desire,
And let your inner flame inspire.

For in this life, we all must learn,
To take a turn and let ourselves yearn,
For the peace that comes with space,
And the freedom to just embrace.

Beautiful Art

You're a beautiful art that came from different pieces of obstacles. Now that you put everything into place, nothing can threaten your being because you know you have your back. You can do this.

You're a masterpiece, a work of art,
Crafted from obstacles that tore you apart,
But you gathered the pieces, put them in place,
And now you stand tall, with confidence and grace.

Your journey was tough, with many trials,
But you persevered, despite the denials,
And now you know, with certainty,
That you are strong, and you can do anything.

You are a painting, with vibrant hues,
A canvas of colors, that tell your truth,
And though you may have once been broken,
You are now whole, and not easily shaken.

You are a sculpture, chiseled and carved,
A symbol of strength, and of all you have survived,
And with each strike of the hammer and chisel,
You emerged, resilient, and unbreakable.

You are a symphony, with many notes,
A beautiful melody, that floats and floats,
And though there may be times of discord,
You know that within you, there is a perfect chord.

So hold your head up high, and know your worth,
For you are a beautiful creation, given birth,
From the challenges and struggles that you've faced,
And now, nothing can threaten your place.

You are a beautiful art, a masterpiece divine,
A shining star, that will always shine,
And no matter what comes your way,
You know you have your back, and you can do this, come what
may.

Nonetheless

Overthinking the things that have happened can hold you back from what is present. You can't take back the things that happened in the past, and you tried many times to make it work; thus, it came to this. Nonetheless, you have felt it all; now, it's just a memory. It doesn't do you good analyzing because you were treated poorly; they did it and knew what they were doing. It doesn't really matter now.

Overthinking, a curse on the mind,
A trap for those who are confined,
To memories of what once was,
A past that can't be changed because,

No matter how hard you may try,
The past can't be undone, no lie,
And yet we ponder and analyze,
Every detail, every surprise.

We dwell on what could have been,
On the pain, on the sin,
We cling to the hurt and the shame,
And in doing so, we lose the game.

For life moves on, it doesn't wait,
It doesn't care about our fate,
And so we must let go and move,
To be present, to find our groove.

We must accept what is now,
And let go of the past somehow,
For the memories, they're just that,
A faded film, a blurry chat.

Don't waste your time on what's done,
On battles that can't be won,
For the past is just a memory,
And it doesn't define your destiny.

So let go of the hurt and pain,
And focus on what you can gain,
For the future is bright and new,
And it's waiting just for you.

Blew

You now focus on what brings you life and have the shine back you've lost since pleasing the wrong people. It's time to stop giving them space in your head more than they deserve. They had the chance, and they blew it.

In the midst of life's chaotic fray,
We lose sight of what brings us true joy each day,
We try to please the masses, to fit in and belong,
And in doing so, we forget where we truly belong.

We give too much space in our minds,
To those who don't deserve our time,
We hold onto hurt and anger,
And in doing so, our own happiness we endanger.

But now it's time to take a stand,
To let go of those who don't understand,
To focus on what brings us life,
And leave behind the pain and strife.

No more wasting energy on those who bring us down,
No more trying to please those who always frown,
Our shine will return, brighter than before,
As we rediscover what we truly adore.

We'll find our place, where we belong,
And in doing so, we'll find the strength to be strong,
For those who had the chance and blew it,
We'll move on, with new purpose and spirit.

So let us focus on what brings us life,
And leave behind those who only bring us strife,
For we deserve to be happy and fulfilled,
And it's time to take back what was once spilled.

Exceptional

You can now do whatever suits you best in your interest. People may notice the change in you; everything seems to fit in the proper place without exerting so much effort. The heaviness you were carrying has lifted, and you now have the joy of a little girl. You deserve to have as many chances as you need to pick yourself up because you're exceptional.

In the depths of despair and the darkest of days
You carried a weight that seemed to never dissipate
But now, a change has come and a shift in your ways
You can do as you please, whatever suits your fate

People have taken notice of the transformation
That has occurred within you, a newfound liberation
Everything seems to fall into its rightful location
No longer a struggle or arduous confrontation

The heaviness that burdened you has finally lifted
A weight that held you down, no longer a weight shifted
Now, the joy of a little girl, so carefree and gifted
You deserved this relief, the weight no longer restricted

You are exceptional, and you deserve to rise again
To pick yourself up, to find the strength within

There is no limit to the chances you can obtain
To find your passion, your purpose, your win

So go forth, with the wind at your back
No longer held down, no longer under attack
The freedom you have found, there is no lack
You are exceptional, and you will stay on track.

Burning Passion

It's easy to get lost track and be passive and do nothing. Lots of questions like, are we here to work and pay bills? Is this the purpose of life? We all have the moment which feels like drowning in an abyss. Keep still, it will pass, and with the help of yourself, you will find your way. Listen to the voice within you where the burning passion would take you. Don't resist. It directs you to your life's fulfillment.

Amidst the hustle and bustle of life's race,
We often lose track of our own pace.
We work and strive to pay our bills,
But in doing so, we forget life's thrills.

Questions arise, like waves in the sea,
Are we merely meant to toil and be?
Do we exist just to earn and survive,
Or is there something more to thrive?

Sometimes we feel like we're drowning,
In life's abyss, it can be astounding.
But if we keep still and hold on tight,
We'll find our way out of the dark night.

In moments like these, we must listen,
To the voice within, it won't be missin'.
It'll guide us to where our passions ignite,
And lead us towards our life's true light.

Don't resist this burning sensation,
It'll guide you to your life's true destination.
You'll find fulfillment in your chosen path,
And leave behind the doubts and aftermath.

So trust yourself and keep moving on,
The journey may be tough, but you're strong.
With the help of yourself, you'll find your way,
And make the most of each and every day.

Amaze Yourself

Your focus can get you years ahead in life. Align what you want and how you see yourself in the future. Don't underestimate yourself; you have the power to make what it takes to be the best version of yourself. Hold on to your desire and be consistent. You'll soon amaze yourself with how you were able to endure moreover exceed what you expected. Don't doubt, you can do it.

In life, there are moments that we find
Our goals seem far and out of mind
We doubt ourselves and wonder why
Our dreams seem distant in our eye

But focus, oh focus, can get us far
It's the light that shines on who we are
Align your wants with your future sight
And watch as your goals come into light

Don't underestimate your own power
You have the strength to climb the highest tower
To be the best version of yourself
Your focus can be your greatest wealth

Hold on tight and be consistent
Your hard work will be so persistent

And soon, you'll amaze yourself
With how you were able to endure, moreover exceed yourself

Don't doubt, don't hesitate
You have the power to create
To be the best that you can be
And live a life that's truly free

So focus on your dreams and goals
And let the fire inside you grow
For with focus and determination
You can achieve your heart's elation.

FOUR

Challenges you face are opportunities to grow and embrace.

Preserve

Finding peace amidst the chaos is the ultimate goal in this kind of society we are living in. You've experienced months of sleepless nights and endless questions swirling in your head that kept you sick of being anxious. Others just don't care and would rather watch you hurt and fall, adding you to their list of victims and naming you another crazy, delusional being. You have to run away from such people to keep your sanity and preserve your well-being.

In this society, chaos reigns supreme,
Leaving us all lost in a waking dream.
With sleepless nights and swirling thoughts,
Anxiety grips us in its vice-like knots.

Like a victim, we're named and shamed,
Delusional, crazy, and falsely blamed.

But we know the truth, we know our worth,
And we won't let their words drag us down to the earth.

Finding peace amidst this chaos is our goal,
A sanctuary for our minds and souls.
We must run from those who don't care,
Who'd rather watch us suffer and despair.

We'll preserve our sanity, our well-being,
And rise above the noise, the hurt, the fleeting.
For in the chaos, there's beauty to be found,
A glimmer of hope, a sight, a sound.

We'll keep our heads up, our hearts strong,
And find the peace that's been missing all along.
For in this society, we'll make our own way,
And find the peace we need to live each day.

Special

All the years you've tried to put the pieces together of a dysfunctional relationship, the work drained you. Finding peace with it all was hard to find; you've tried all sorts to find your way through. Finally, you've come to terms with cutting off the weeds surrounding your heart from pricking the life from you. Realize that no one is worth sacrificing your peace for. Nonetheless, the time and energy it takes to reach internal peace should never be compromised for those who won't go the extra mile, let alone lift a finger for you. Remember, you are special too.

In the labyrinth of love, you wandered astray
Trying to put the pieces in place, every day
A dysfunctional relationship you tried to mend
But the energy it drained, felt like the end

You searched high and low for a way out
Hoping to find peace, without a doubt
All sorts of methods you tried, to no avail
The heart-wrenching pain, you couldn't curtail

But finally, you found the strength to cut off the weeds
The ones that pricked your heart, making it bleed

You realized that no one is worth your peace
And letting go of toxic love, was the key to release

The time and energy it takes to find internal peace
Should never be compromised, for those who don't cease
To hurt you, let alone lift a finger for your sake
Remember, you are special, and your heart deserves a break

So let the winds of change blow away the past
And let your heart heal, with love that will last
For you are worthy of a love that's true
A love that lifts you up, and makes you feel anew.

Stop

Having to stand up for yourself was the best thing you did for yourself, and I am proud of you. Yes, you have a big heart, for you've endured the different abuse and manipulation they inflicted on you. You think it was normal because you've grown accustomed to it all. However, you got so exhausted that you needed to explode. Their time is up; they have used all their chances in you. You have to stop at some point.

A heart so big, it's easy to see,
Endured abuse and manipulation, relentlessly.
Thinking it was normal, growing accustomed to the pain,
But the time has come to break the chain.

Standing up for oneself, not an easy task,
But you did it, and I'm proud, bask
In the glow of self-love and courage,
For you've extinguished the fire of outrage.

Exhausted and tired, you needed to explode,
To let out the emotion that had been bestowed.
Their time is up, they've used all their chances,
No more opportunities, no more false romances.

It takes strength to say enough is enough,
But now you can pick yourself up.
You're not alone, you have support,
And your own self-worth to report.

Having to stand up for yourself,
Was the best thing, and it's not a shelf,
You'll continue to grow and thrive,
And in the end, you'll surely survive.

Your Heart

You became strong and courageous to move past that chapter of your life. Your heart was ripped apart beyond repair. Moreover, you've been let down by the ones you love most, but that did not scare you. Nevertheless, you still get out of bed and go through everyday challenges.

You were once shattered, torn apart,
Your heart in pieces, a broken heart.
The chapter of your life, so dark and bleak,
But you stood up and refused to be weak.

You were let down by those you love,
Their broken promises like a glove.
But you did not falter, you did not fall,
You stood tall, you stood strong through it all.

Your courage, a beacon in the night,
A shining star, a guiding light.
You moved past the pain, the hurt, the strife,
Through every challenge, you fought for your life.

Your heart may be damaged, but it's not beyond repair,
You find strength in yourself, a warrior, fierce and rare.
You wake up each day, with a heart full of grace,
Ready to conquer anything, to face any race.

Your journey has not been easy, it's true,
But your unwavering spirit, your resilience, shines through.
You are a fighter, a survivor, a champion of life,
Moving forward, with faith, hope, and a heart full of light.

A Survivor

The person you've become has a depth that no one would know. A person who understands but is misunderstood, kind-hearted though tough, has fears but is brave. You've turned out to be a survivor.

The person you've become, oh what a mystery!
A depth that no one could ever see,
Understood by few, misunderstood by many,
Kind-hearted yet tough, remarkable aplenty.

You've faced your fears with courage in your heart,
And turned out to be a survivor from the start,
Your battles fought with tenacity and grit,
A story of triumph that can never be quit.

The weight of the world on your shoulders you bore,
Yet your spirit remained unbroken to its very core,
The scars you wear, a testament to your might,
A proof of your struggles and your endless fight.

Misjudged and underestimated, you stand tall,
A force to be reckoned with, through it all,
You've learned to be gentle, yet fierce when need be,
A person of substance, a rarity to see.

The person you've become, a work of art,
A masterpiece that's only just begun to start,
So keep on shining, warrior, like a star,
For you're a survivor, no matter how far.

Define

Your past doesn't define who you are. You are not the things that happened to you or the people who treated you poorly. What happened has happened and you can't turn around and change it. Accept and be grateful that you have surpassed the trial. It is now in history that you've greatly learned for your future. You've gone through different challenges threatening to destroy you and the people waiting for your failure.

In the past, you may have suffered,
Experienced pain, and felt deterred.
People may have treated you poorly,
And you may have felt sad and lonely.

But know this, dear one, it's not your identity,
You are so much more than your past and its severity.
The events that happened, they cannot define you,
You've gone through them, and now, they're through.

Be grateful for the trials and tribulations,
They're the marks of your life and its revelations,
The hurdles you've jumped, the hurdles ahead,
All part of the journey, in this life you're led.

You've overcome challenges, big and small,
And with each victory, you stand tall,
The people waiting for your failure,
They see you rise, and they grow paler.

For you, dear one, are a survivor,
Your strength, your will, they're a driver,
To greatness, to a future so bright,
Where you'll shine, like a star in the night.

So don't let the past hold you down, I
t's not what you are or what you're bound,
You're free to create and to be who you want,
To live life fully, without any taunt.

You've learned so much from your history,
And the future, it's now a mystery,
But you can face it with courage and might,
For you've proven that you can fight.

So hold your head up, and walk with pride,
For you're a warrior, and you've survived,
The past is gone, and the future's near,
Embrace it, dear one, without any fear.

Unfazed

You needed all the bitter things to appreciate and rise above all the chaos and disruptions along your way. With the process, you're changing into someone even better while moving forward toward your beautiful future. Your experiences taught you how to be unmoved in times of trials, and your soul would remain unfazed by what could disrupt your balance.

In life's journey, we oftentimes find
That hurdles and obstacles leave us
behind We strive and struggle to make our way
Through chaos and disruptions every day

But as we journey through the bitter things
Our souls are strengthened by the lessons they bring
We learn to rise above the trials we face
And move forward with a sense of grace
For every bump and every fall

Has taught us how to stand up tall
We've learned to be unmoved in times of strife
And remain unfazed by the storms of life
These experiences have molded us anew

And changed us into someone better, it's true
We've grown beyond our past selves' measure
And are moving towards our beautiful future's treasure

So let the bitter things come our way
For we know they'll help us rise above the fray
And lead us towards a brighter tomorrow
Where our souls can soar free from all sorrow.

Potential

Alas, you are no longer the person you were yesterday. The lesson from your past that taught you courage and wisdom is now what you carry in your heart with much potential. You are the exact person you're meant to be.

Alas, dear wanderer, you've changed,
No longer the same as yesterday's range,
You carry the lesson from past to present age,
Courage and wisdom, your heart's new page.

The person you were, now a distant memory,
A mere reflection of a former legacy,
But fear not, for this change is meant to be,
Embrace it, for it sets you free. T

he fire within now burns so bright,
Illuminating the path, once shrouded in night,
With newfound strength, you take flight,
Unleashing your potential with all your might.

The future awaits, the world is your stage,
With every step, you leave behind the cage,
No longer bound by fear and rage,
For you are the person meant to turn the page.

So go forth, dear wanderer, with head held high,
Let your courage and wisdom light up the sky,
Embrace the change, as time passes by,
For you are the exact person, meant to fly.

Focus

There is a time for everything; each baby steps are necessary for the process. Keep your focus on what you're aiming for. Don't let anyone shake your reality; they may criticize, ridicule, or doubt you. Nevertheless, let them know you have better things to do for your greatness of yourself than to listen to their ridiculous chants. They are just holding you back, which you don't want to waste your time with.

There is a time for everything, they say
Each step, each move, each breath, day by day
Is necessary for the process to unfold
As we grasp and strive to reach our goal

But amidst the journey, we may find
That some try to shake our minds
Critics, doubters, and those who ridicule
Their words may cause our spirit to dwindle

Yet, we must keep our focus on what we aim
For our greatness, our purpose, our claim to fame
We cannot let their chants deter us from our path
Or allow them to drag us down in their wrath

We must let them know that we have better things to do
Than to listen to their negativity that makes us blue
They are merely holding us back from our potential
And we won't waste our time with their detrimental rumble

So let us take each baby step with great care
As we move forward, our dreams we shall bear
For there is a time for everything, it's true
And we shall reach our destination, me and you.

Believe

Keep doing your best; it might not have yet been written. Thus, you'll get there. Let life take its course, don't force what's not yet supposed to happen, for it will eventually unfold itself. Moreover, it will happen when it's time. Look at the direction of the prize and follow through. Believe in yourself. That's where your power is.

In life's great game, we strive for fame,
To win the prize and take our claim,
But oftentimes, we feel the strain,
Our efforts lost, our hopes in vain.

Don't despair, my friend, or lose your zest,
For what's important is to do your best,
Though your path may be unclear,
Keep pushing on, don't give in to fear.

The road may wind, and twist, and turn,
And at times, it may seem we'll never learn,
But trust the journey, let it unfold,
For each step, a story waiting to be told.

The future is not yet written,
But with each move, a new page is smitten,

So keep your eyes on the prize ahead,
And believe in yourself, no matter what's said.

Life will take its own sweet time,
And what's meant to be will fall in line,
So don't force what's not yet due,
For it will happen when it's time for you.

Believe in your power, and let it shine,
For in your heart, the victory is divine,
And with each step, you'll find your way,
To the place where dreams come to stay.

Fair Enough

Not everybody understands you, and that's fine. They might think you're a complex person and not their cup of tea, but that's fair enough. However, don't be a people pleaser just to have someone you can call a friend or hubby; you're better than that. Stop chasing anyone and trying to be liked so you can belong. That would soon backfire on you, and it would cut deep.

In a world of varied thought,
Not every soul perceives the same.
Some see a work of art,
While others simply see a frame.

You are a person of depth,
Complexity is your name.
You may not be everyone's cup of tea,
But that is not your shame.

Do not be a people pleaser,
Just to have someone near.
You deserve more than a mere friend or hubby,
Settle not for something that's insincere.

Stop chasing the elusive "like",
For the sake of being part of the throng.

It will soon
lead to a life of strife,
And leave you feeling alone and wronged.

Believe in yourself, my dear,
Your worth is not tied to another's view.
Embrace your complexity, without fear,
And let your true colors shine through.

For those who don't understand,
Let them be, let them go their way.
You are not meant for everyone,
But that's okay, be proud and stay.

In the end, it's not about fitting in,
But about staying true to who you are.
Don't sacrifice your soul to win,
For it will leave a lifelong scar.

So be yourself, embrace your complexity,
And let the world see the real you.
Don't settle for a life of insincerity,
For you deserve a life that's true.

Phantom

You are extraordinary; others might find it hard to navigate your thoughts because of your depth, passion, and uniqueness. These may be hard to phantom for small-minded people; thus, you don't have to exert your time explaining. You know exactly who you are, that is all that matters, and it's okay if they don't. If they were your people, they would try to understand you. However, if they are conditioned to being shallow, your depth will always be intimidating.

You are a soul of deep vastness,
An ocean of thoughts, a universe of passion,
A unique entity, an extraordinary being,
With depths which are hard to fathom.

Small-minded folks find it hard to navigate,
Through the maze of your intricate thoughts,
And your depth can be intimidating,
For those who are conditioned to being shallow.

Your depth, passion, and uniqueness,
Are a testament to your strength and resilience,
And should be celebrated as the treasures they are,
For they make you who you are, extraordinary, and rare.

You know who you are, and that's all that matters,
Your uniqueness sets you apart from the crowd,
And if they were your people, they would try to understand,
The intricate weave of your thoughts, that make you stand
out.

So, let them be, those who cannot see your brilliance,
For you shine brighter than the stars in the sky,
And only those who are worthy will seek your depths,
And appreciate the beauty, that makes you fly.

But fret not, dear soul, for you need not explain,
To those who cannot see beyond the surface level,
For they will not understand the beauty,
Of the depth, you possess, and the passion you revel.

Frequency

Your light shines through, and it reaches the ones who vibrate on the same frequency as yours. It calms your soul and keeps your peace. The times when you got ignored because they were having bad days or treated you like a burden because they couldn't find their worth along the way is now over. Don't blame yourself. You did not deserve it.

With each passing day, your light glows bright,
A beacon of warmth that shines through the night,
And it reaches those who match your frequency,
Those who feel the same, those who keep you company.

It's a soothing presence that calms your soul,
A peaceful energy that makes you whole,
And though there were times you were overlooked,
Ignored like a book, or pushed aside like a crook,

Those days are gone now, they're in the past,
Don't hold onto them, they don't have to last,
For you are worthy, deserving of love,
And those who can't see it, they're not above,

The power of your light, the beauty you possess,
So don't blame yourself, don't feel any distress,

For they were having bad days, lost in their own strife,
But your light still shines, bringing warmth to your life.

So let it shine bright, let it fill you up,
And know that you're enough, that you're more than enough,
For your light shines through, and it reaches far,
Guiding you on your journey, like a shining star.

Should Be

You've been through the worst, so it won't be as hard to go through it again. It would still be uncomfortable and hurtful while going through, though it wouldn't be as invasive as much. There would still be a breaking point, but you'll heal faster this time and knows a better path to go to. You know that holding resentments would lengthen your misery. You've learned to forgive and accept things as they should be.

Through the worst, you've been before
And though it hurts, you know the score
For though discomfort may remain
You know your strength, it's not in vain

The breaking point, it comes again
But now you know a better zen
You'll heal much faster, this you know
And find a path that helps you grow

Resentments, they will keep you down
The misery they bring, will wear your crown
Forgiveness is the way to go
Acceptance leads to a better flow

It's not to say it won't be hard
For pain and struggle, they're on guard
But with your knowledge, strength, and skill
You'll face the worst and climb the hill

So hold your head up, don't give in
For though the road may seem so grim
You've been through worst, you know the score
And now you're stronger than before.

Peace

The peace that took over you was the result of all the experiences you've endured. You have a better understanding of how to deal with upheaval when presented to you. You've grown from sacrifices and have your head held high, for you've come to know your worth.

The peace that took over you is not so simple,
A product of all the trials you've been through;
The road you've traveled has been far from gentle,
And yet you've learned how to endure and renew.

The upheavals that once would have left you shaken,
Now only serve to strengthen your resolve;
The sacrifices you've made have not been forsaken,
And on them, you've built yourself to evolve.

You've come to know the worth of your own being,
To value all that makes you who you are;
And though the path you've walked has not been freeing,
You hold your head up high, as you're now a star.

For all the darkness that you've faced and conquered,
Has only served to make you stronger still;
And now your light shines bright, unencumbered,
A beacon of hope, a testament to will.

So let the peace that took over you be a reminder,
Of all that you've endured and overcome;
For though the journey was rough, you're a survivor,
And in your heart, you know you've truly won.

Lifetime

You might not know how amazing you are. The way you present yourself to the world, how you carry your conversations, the kindness you give to people who needs it, and the smile you share, even though it's momentarily can last a lifetime to some who most need to be seen.

You might not know how amazing you are,
How the world brightens up when you're not afar,
The way you speak, the words you share,
Can light up someone's day, show them you care.

The kindness you give so selflessly,
Can heal a heart that's broken and empty,
The smile you share, even if it's brief,
Can bring joy to someone's life, beyond belief.

Your presence alone can shift the mood,
Make everything feel a little less crude,
Your actions may seem small and insignificant,
But they can have an impact that's truly magnificent.

You might not know how much you mean,
How much you influence and intervene,
The world needs people like you, who shine,
Who bring light and hope, and make life divine.

So don't underestimate your worth,
For you are a treasure on this earth,
Keep shining bright, keep being you,
For the world needs more people like you.

Greatness

Spreading love makes the world a little less hard to live. Though sometimes, the outside noise makes you unstable, and seeing others barely getting through while carrying their crosses leaves a big question of purpose. Continue to have a heart with a good deal of pure intentions. You're not expecting something in return thus, the world knows how to give back good karma. Reminding yourself of whom you've become and consistently being grounded have the highest pull of energy. And considering that you're having struggles as well, keep your greatness. That makes you beautiful.

Spreading love, a noble quest,
Making life a little less hard to digest,
But the outside noise, it can weigh you down,
Leaving you feeling unstable and bound.

Seeing others barely getting through,
Carrying their crosses, a purpose in view,
It leaves you with a question in mind,
What is your purpose, what must you find?

Have a heart, pure intentions in tow,
Not expecting anything in return, go with the flow,
The world knows how to give back what you sow,
Good karma, it will come, let it grow.

Remind yourself of who you've become,
Stay grounded, focus, let the drumbeat of your heart not
become undone,
Consistently being in tune with your inner voice,
It's the highest pull of energy, it's your choice.

And in your struggles, keep your greatness,
For that alone, makes you beautiful, with no need for any
witness,
Spread love, be kind, and give what you can,
For in the end, it's the legacy you leave, the ultimate plan.

Honestly

You were allowing them to continue to have a hold on you, even though you had already moved on. You let them continue to have a say in your life, even though they had no right to do so. You allowed them to continue to be present in your life, even though they had already left it. Finally, you realized that to move on honestly, you had to let go of your anger, bitterness, and resentment towards those who had hurt you.

You were holding on to the past, a prisoner to your pain,
Allowing them to have a hold, your life they would constrain.
Though you'd already moved on, your heart still held a weight,
Their words and actions lingered, a constant mental state.

You let them have a say, in how you lived your life,
Though they had no right, to add to all your strife.
You let them stay present, though they'd already left,
Their memory a burden, a weight upon your chest.

But finally you realized, to be free you must release,
The anger, bitterness, and resentment, your soul they did
fleece.
A weight lifted off your shoulders, you felt a sense of peace,
The hold they had on you, finally did cease.

No longer a prisoner, you could live your life anew,
The pain of the past, no longer did it ensue.
You had the power within, to let go and move on,
And in doing so, your heart became strong.

So if you find yourself in pain, let go of the weight,
Release the anger, bitterness, and the hate.
For only then can you truly be free,
And live the life you were always meant to be.

My Own

I had to take back my peace and make it my own. I had to take back my joy and make it my own. I had to take back my happiness and make it my own. I had to take back my life and make it my own. I had to let go of the anger, bitterness, and resentment toward those who hurt me to move on. I had to take back my life and make it my own. I had to take back my freedom and make it my own.

Within my soul, a storm once brewed,
My peace and joy held captive, subdued.
Happiness seemed a distant dream,
My life, no longer mine, it seemed.

But then one day, I saw with clarity,
That only I could control my destiny.
No longer would I let pain define me,
I had to take back what was rightfully mine, you see.

My peace, my joy, my happiness too,
I had to reclaim them, start anew.
I had to let go of bitterness and hate,
To move forward, to create my fate.

So I took back my life, piece by piece,
My freedom, my will, my heart at ease.
For only I can choose my path,
And in this realization, I found my strength at last.

Now I stand tall, my spirit unbroken,
My past a memory, no longer a token.
I am the master of my own fate,
I took back my life, and made it great.

In Life

Letting go can be one of the most challenging things to do in life. It can be hard to let go of people, places, and things a person has grown to love and cherish. It can be hard to let go of the past and move on to the future. Moreover, letting go of dreams and ambitions and accepting the reality of a current situation can be hard due to expectations and the uncertainty of the future. It is a process that requires being honest with oneself and accepting the things that cannot change.

Letting go, a challenge we all must face,
A journey through life's uncharted space,
With people, places, and things we adore,
To release our grip, and love them no more.

The past, a weight that we carry along,
Memories that we can never be wrong,
But time, an ever-moving tide,
Washes away what we try to hide.

Dreams and ambitions, we hold so tight,
A vision of the future, that shines so bright,
But reality can be a bitter pill,
A truth, we must accept, despite the thril

Expectations, a burden we all bear,
A weight that we willingly share,
But the future, an enigma we cannot see,
We must let go, and let our hearts be free.

Letting go, a process that demands,
Honesty and courage to understand,
Accepting what we cannot change,
Embracing the future, without restraint.

For in the end, it's not what we hold,
But what we release, that makes us bold,
To wander the world, with an open heart,
And let go of all that keeps us apart.

Contentment

On the other hand, it opens new possibilities when willing to take chances. Letting go is a journey that can be both a painful yet liberating, complex process and a rewarding one. It can help a person grow and become stronger and wiser to appreciate the present moment and live life to the fullest. Which ultimately brings peace and contentment to one's life. Letting go is a choice to make, accept the things that cannot change, and move forward with courage and hope. Finally, it is a choice to be open to new possibilities, take risks, and trust that things will work out.

On the other hand, it opens new possibilities
When willing to take chances, with great abilities
Letting go of the past, a journey begun
A painful yet liberating, complex process, but it can be fun

Like a butterfly emerging from its cocoon
Letting go is a transformation that happens soon
A metamorphosis of the mind and soul
A rebirth of oneself, making the person whole

Letting go can be a struggle, no doubt
Fear and doubt may creep in and cause a pout

But with each step forward, a person grows
Stronger and wiser, embracing the highs and the lows

Letting go can be rewarding, that's for sure
Like a treasure found, it can be a great lure
Peace and contentment to one's life it brings
Living life to the fullest, spreading the wings

Letting go is a choice that we make
Accepting things that cannot change, no more fake
Moving forward with courage and hope
Creating a life with a beautiful scope

Being open to new possibilities, taking risks
Trusting that things will work out, no more tricks
Chasing dreams, no matter how far
The possibilities are endless, like a shining star

In conclusion, letting go is a journey worth taking
A complex process, but the end is worth making
It brings peace, contentment, and a life fulfilled
Letting go is a choice, a choice we can build.